First World War
and Army of Occupation
War Diary
France, Belgium and Germany

33 DIVISION
Divisional Troops
167 Brigade Royal Field Artillery
20 April 1915 - 11 September 1916

WO95/2413/6

The Naval & Military Press Ltd
www.nmarchive.com
Published in association with The National Archives

Published by

The Naval & Military Press Ltd

Unit 10 Ridgewood Industrial Park,

Uckfield, East Sussex,

TN22 5QE England

Tel: +44 (0) 1825 749494

www.naval-military-press.com

www.nmarchive.com

This diary has been reprinted in facsimile from the original. Any imperfections are inevitably reproduced and the quality may fall short of modern type and cartographic standards.

© Crown Copyright
Images reproduced by permission of The National Archives, London, England, 2015.

Contents

Document type	Place/Title	Date From	Date To
Heading	WO95/2413/6		
Heading	33rd Division Divl Artillery 167th Brigade R.F.A. Jan-Sep 1916		
Heading	33 167 R.F.A. Vol 2		
Heading	33rd Div 167th Bde. R.F.A. Vol I		
War Diary	Grove Vale East-Dulwich	20/04/1915	30/04/1915
War Diary	East-Dulwich Barhs	01/05/1915	03/05/1915
War Diary	East Dulwich	04/05/1915	07/08/1915
War Diary	Bulford	08/08/1915	09/08/1915
War Diary	Bulford Camp	18/08/1915	15/09/1915
War Diary	Bulford	18/09/1915	25/10/1915
War Diary	Bulford Camp	27/10/1915	30/11/1915
War Diary	Dev	01/12/1915	07/12/1915
War Diary	Bulford	08/12/1915	17/12/1915
War Diary	Berguette	18/12/1915	29/02/1916
War Diary	Annequin	01/03/1916	29/04/1916
War Diary	In The Field	11/05/1916	31/05/1916
War Diary	France	01/06/1916	30/06/1916
Heading	War Diary Headquarters, 167th Brigade R.F.A. July 1916		
War Diary	Cuinchy Sector	05/07/1916	31/07/1916
Heading	Appendices I. II. III. IIIA & IV.		
Miscellaneous	O.C. A.B.C./167 Appendix I		
Miscellaneous			
Miscellaneous	Bombardment Orders Appendix II		
Miscellaneous	167 Brigade Order		
Miscellaneous	A.B.C./167 Appendix III	26/07/1916	26/07/1916
Miscellaneous	Appendix IIIA		
Miscellaneous	167 Brigade Order	26/07/1916	26/07/1916
Miscellaneous	Ref. 53 DA BM/5/507	27/07/1916	27/07/1916
Map	Map No. X5		
Miscellaneous	Appendix IV		
Miscellaneous	167 Bde Order	30/07/1916	30/07/1916
Heading	33rd Divisional Artillery 167th Brigade Royal Field Artillery August 1916		
War Diary		01/08/1916	30/08/1916
Heading	Headquarters 33rd Divinl Artillery		
War Diary		01/09/1916	11/09/1916

WO95/2413(6)

33RD DIVISION
DIVL ARTILLERY

167TH BRIGADE R.F.A.
JAN-SEP 1916

BROKEN UP

33

167 RFA

Vol 2

167ᵗʰ Bde. BPg.
Vol: I

121/7910

33 ᵗᵘᵈ Bis

WAR DIARY or INTELLIGENCE SUMMARY

Army Form C. 2118

167th Brigade R.F.A. Vol. I

Place	Date	Hour	Summary of Events and Information	Remarks and references to Appendices
Grove Vale East Dulwich	20.4.15	—	167th (Howitzer) Brigade R.F.A. Formation of Unit authorised by London District Order No. 138 of June 15th 1915. (C.R.L.D. 702 46138)(W.O.20/Artillery/3838(A61) 30.4.1915.	
—	21.4.15		108 Recruits joined (93 billeted at home and 15 billeted out by Civil Police.	
—	22.4.15		22 Recruits joined (with above posted to "A" Battery 167th Bde R.F.A.) 100 Recruits joined (98 billeted at home & 24 billeted out)	
—	23.4.15		10 Recruits joined completing "B" Battery to 110 men.} 100 Billeted at home 113 — " — to "C" Battery. } 13 — " — out. Lieut. Fallen joined and took over Adjutant of 167th Bde R.F.A. & of Gazette 9.4.15. All men found amongst recruits joined with a previous knowledge of drills were given squads of 50 for Marching and Physical Drills under the supervision of Lieut. Winterls 166th Bde R.F.A. and Sergt-Major Larkin 156th Bde R.F.A.	
—	24.4.15		16 Recruits joined, posted to "C" Battery, completing that battery to 129 men 20 — " — — " — — " — to "B" — " — — " — — " — 113 — " — 65 — " — — " — — " — to "D" — " — — " — — " — 65 — " — 130 " C 91 Billeted at home, 10 billeted out.	

WAR DIARY
or
INTELLIGENCE SUMMARY

(2)

167th (Howitzer) Bde R.F.A.

Place	Date	Hour	Summary of Events and Information	Remarks and references to Appendices
Grove Vale East Dulwich	26/4/15		65 Recruits joined, posted to "D" Battery completing their battery to 130 men. 48 — " — , — " — , — " — to Bde Amm. Column. (82 Billeted at home, 31 billeted out).	
— " —	27/4/15		118 Recruits joined, posted to Bde A.C. } 138 Billeted at home 35 — " — — " — to Bde Hdqrs Staff — } 15 Billeted out	
— " —	28/4/15		Owing to congestion on Dog Kennel Hill Drill ground, the 167th Bde R.F.A moved from Grove Vale Depot to Public Baths at East Dulwich, giving the Baths, Goose Green, and Peckham Rye for drill purposes. Drills carried out, Marching, Physical Training, Semaphore Signalling, and Knotting & Lashing.	
East Dulwich Baths	1.5.15		Divisional Arty Parade. 167th Bde R.F.A. in plain clothes dismounted march past on Peckham Rye for Recruiting purposes to complete 126th Heavy Battery R.G.A. and 33 fd hist Arty Ammn Column.	
— " —	3.5.15		Public Baths at East Dulwich taken over from London County Council. Report of breakages taken and forwarded to Treasurer Town Hall Camberwell.	

WAR DIARY
or
INTELLIGENCE SUMMARY
(Erase heading not required.)

Army Form C. 2118

(3)

1/4th (Howitzer) Bde R.F.A. Summary of Events and Information

Place	Date	Hour	Summary of Events and Information	Remarks and references to Appendices
East Dulwich	4.5.15		Organisation of Battery & Brigade Offices in living rooms of Public Baths, and allotment of places for storage of Clothing and equipment. This building containing two large plunge baths boarded over was found very suitable for drilling purposes during inclement weather, and later when equipped, for housing two thirds of the Brigade, ie, 80 men who were billeted over a scattered area of London districts. Two Battery Sergt. majors joined and attached for instructional purposes one posted to "A" Bty, the other to "B" Battery	
— " —	5.5.15		One B.S. major attached as instructor and posted to "C" Battery. Lieut. F.W. Price joined and was posted to "A" Battery. (date of Gazette 21-4-15). Contract made with Mr A Keen Hunt, 1 Brampton Street S.E. to repair boots. Many men enlisted very poorly clothed and with bad boots which impeded their instruction in marching drills etc.	
— " —	6.5.15		One Sergt. joined as Instructor, posted to "D" Battery.	
— " —	7.5.15		5 men selected for Signalling instruction under Sergt Ash 156th Brigade RFA. French & German Language classes started at East Dulwich Baths between 5.30pm and 7pm. Lessons given by Ladies under the direction of Lady Bathurst, two days per week.	

Army Form C. 2118

WAR DIARY
or
INTELLIGENCE SUMMARY

(Erase heading not required.)

Instructions regarding War Diaries and Intelligence Summaries are contained in F.S. Regs., Part II. and the Staff Manual respectively. Title Pages will be prepared in manuscript.

(3a)

Place	Date	Hour	Summary of Events and Information	Remarks and references to Appendices
East Enbirk	8.5.15	5	167th Howitzer Bde R.F.A. recruits joined and posted to "A" Battery	Billeted at Home
		5	— " — — " — — " — B — " —	10 Billeted at home 2 Billeted out
— " —	10.5.15	12	— " — — " — — " — C — " —	Billeted at home
		7	— " — — " — — " — B — " —	— " —
— " —		10	— " — — " — — " — "D" — " —	— " — 1 billeted out
		10	— " — — " — — " — Bde Amm Colum	9 — " — 1 — " —
— " —	11.5.15	2	— " — — " — — " — D Battery	1 — " — 1 — " —
— " —		1	— " — — " — — " — Bde A.C.	Billeted at home

WAR DIARY
or
INTELLIGENCE SUMMARY

Army Form C. 2118

(4) 164th Brigade R.F.A.

Place	Date	Hour	Summary of Events and Information	Remarks and references to Appendices
East Dulwich	8.5.15		3 men promoted to Corpl. 1 man to Bombr. and 28 appointed Unpaid A.Bombrs. for disciplinary purposes. Owing to all men being in plain clothes the following method of distinction was adopted. Bombrs. "White Arm Band." Corpls. "Blue", and Sergts. "Red".	
— " —	10.5.15		2 Bombdrs & 2 Sergts. joined for duty as Instructors, as posted as follows. 1 Bomr. to "A" Bty. & 1 to "B" Bty. 1 Sergt. to "A" Bty. & 1 Sergt. to Bde Amm. Column.	
— " —	13.5.15		Lieut. C.E. Lane joined and posted to "B" Battery. Date of Gazette 26-4-15. First consignment of Clothing and Necessaries received from Wheeler & Co. Poultry London. First consignment of Bedding & Barrack utensils received from Tower of London. This latter consignment being the first arrangement made for house men at the Baths. A good number of men were billeted so far from place of assembly, drills between the hours of 9.15.12 and 2.6.5pm could only be carried out.	
— " —	15.5.15		1 BS Major joined for duty as Instructor. Posted to "D" Battery.	
— " —	19.5.15		20 men sent to School of Instruction at Bermondsey for Course of Cold Shoeing. 1st issue of Clothing & necessaries made to house men. Clothing was fitted by Contractor "Wheeler & Co." Divisional Ceremonial Parade on Peckham Rye. Officers mounted.	
— " —	20.5.15		Lieut. R.N.T. Huggins joined and posted to "C" Bty. Date of Gazette 6-5-15.	

WAR DIARY or INTELLIGENCE SUMMARY

Army Form C. 2118

16th Brigade R.F.A.

Place	Date	Hour	Summary of Events and Information	Remarks and references to Appendices
Goathurst	24.5.15		Lieut W. Bowden Smith joined and posted to "D" Battery. Date of Gazette 9-6-15.	
"	29.5.15		Map Reading course commenced for Officers at Grove Vale Depot. 23 Horses received from 156th Bde R.F.A. and riding lessons commenced. 2 Dummy Howitzers received and Gun Drill instruction started.	
"	31.5.15		Ceremonial Parade on Peckham Rye and Inspection by Inspector General of Horse & Field Artillery. By this date two Batteries were equipped with Clothing & Necessaries.	
"	3.6.15		Lieut. G.E. Lane proceeded to Dunstable for course Telephony.	
"	4.6.15		"D"/B Batteries paraded at King's College Hospital for Inoculation (1st).	
"	5.6.15		Lieut. J.J. King joined and posted to "B" Battery. Date of Gazette 5.6.15. C & D Batteries paraded at King's College Hospital for Inoculation (1st). C & D Batteries issued with Clothing (dated) and Necessaries.	
"	10.6.15		1. Staff Sgt Farrier joined for Instructional purposes and posted to 13th Amm. Column.	
"	11.6.15		A Lantern Lecture on "Wound Infection and Infectious diseases" was given to the Brigade at the Tower Cinema Theatre by Research Defence Society.	
"	14.6.15		5 men sent on Cookery Course at Lords Cricket-Ground School of Cookery.	

WAR DIARY or INTELLIGENCE SUMMARY

Army Form C. 2118

6/ 1st Bde. R.F.A.

Place	Date	Hour	Summary of Events and Information	Remarks and references to Appendices
East Dulwich	15/6/15		450 N.C.O.s & men taken from "Billets" the greatest distance from Baths and quartered in that building. Booking of food arranged by using Gas Stoves, 1 travelling cooker shot. Camp kettles. Fire drill and precautions arranged. Orders issued re Barrack discipline. Application made for Separation allowances for married men brought into Barracks. Orderly Officer detailed to sleep in building.	
-,,-	16/6/15		2nd Inoculation of N.C.O. & men completed (Percentage Inoculated 97°)	
-,,-	21/6/15		Lieut W.B. Petts sent on a course of Telephony at Woolwich.	
-,,-	15/6/15		Saddlery & Harness received from Woolwich. Programme of Drills ordered. Gunnery Lectures in Public Baths. Skeleton Drill & Skeleton Driving Drill on Goose Green (Knotting, Lashing, Physical Drill & Skeleton Driving Drill on the Line of march (Stable management, Care of horses in Stables and saddlery) In Bailey's Yard where fitting & cleaning of Harness and saddlery) horses were billeted. Riding Drill at Grove Vale Depôt grounds & on Peckham Rye.	
-,,-	28/6/15		Lieut A.S. Donald joined and posted to "A" Battery said to be gazetted 17-4-13	

WAR DIARY or INTELLIGENCE SUMMARY

Army Form C. 2118

167th Bde. R.F.A.

Place	Date	Hour	Summary of Events and Information	Remarks and references to Appendices
East Dulwich	26.6.15		Lieut. J.G.B. Gardner joined and posted to B.&C.A.C. Date of Gazette 23-6-15.	
"	30.6.15		9 men transferred to 156th Bde R.F.A. for Divisional Arty Board. The whole of the Brigade clothed and issued with necessaries and accoutrements.	
"	5.7.15		Lieut. A. Haythornthwaite joined & posted to "B" By. Date of Gazette 5-3-15. 167th Bde 4 Amn wagons, 1 Telephone Cart & 1 Cooker Division Route march. 38 Single Riders turned out, the remainder were with teams. The above was the 1st parade with Vehicles. Dismounted.	
"	12.7.15		Lieut. G.E. Lane to Larkhill for course of Gunnery (Howitzer)	
"	16.7.15		Lieut. A. Klove joined. Posted to "D" Battery. Date of Gazette	
"	20.7.15		Lieut. E. Parker-Jones joined. Posted to C. Battery. Inspection of Horses by A.D.V.S, London Dist.	
"	26.7.15		Lieut. S.H. Purdey joined from 156th Bde R.F.A. and posted to "B" Battery. 12- 4.5" Q.F. Howitzers received.	

WAR DIARY or INTELLIGENCE SUMMARY

Army Form C. 2118

164th Bde R.F.a.

Place	Date	Hour	Summary of Events and Information	Remarks and references to Appendices
East Bulford	27/7/15		Practice in entrainment of horses & vehicles.	
"	30/7/15		Advance Party of 2 Officers 50 NCOs & men proceeded from Bulford to Bulford.	
"	"		2nd Q.F. 4.5" Howitzer received.	
"	1.8.15		Lieut S.H. Sunday to Signal Depot Dunstable for course of Telephony.	
"	2.8.15		2 Guns & 587 Howitzers received. (Total 4, one issued to each Battery).	
"	6.8.15		Lieut. S.G. Taylor joined & posted to "C" Battery.	
"	7.8.15		Brigade moved between the the hours of 9pm to 11am 8.8.15 from Waterloo Station to Bulford. Journey to Waterloo from Bulford by Road.	
Bulford	8.8.15		Arrival at new Station No. 9 Camp Bulford.	
"	9.8.15		Lieuts E.P. Jones, H. Roland, L.B. Gardner, & S.S. Taylor to Larkhill S.o.G. for Course of Gunnery (Howitzer).	

WAR DIARY
INTELLIGENCE SUMMARY

Army Form C. 2118

Place	Date	Hour	Summary of Events and Information	Remarks and references to Appendices
Bulford Camp	18th Aug	—	L/Col S/John Platt Taylor S.S.O. arrived to take over Command. Reports to Brig. Genl. R.A.	
	19"	—	Officers men starts this day.	
			Routine — inspecting units — lectures to officers.	
	20"	—	Commenced giving drill to officers — lecture officers.	
	21"	—	Recruits came in. Maj. Sc--- who charged --	
	22"	—	Chief Inde. Inspected Genl. Sneah. Not a certain of the Recruits.	
	23"	—	Giving Drill — Lecture Officers	
	24"	—	" Kote inspection. 50 Recruits arrived. There are a number of Army worms in the tents & encampment must be carefully inspected. Hay & Straw Loads to C Battery.	
			S.S.O. arrived & form. Posts to C Battery.	
	26"	—	Sent 24 M.D. horses to T.H.S.C. —	
			40 remounts posted from TIDWORTH Sept —	
	28"	—	1 Sept. 1 Capt. Sp. Res. posted from 3(R) Res. Brigade.	
	29"	—	Capt Steel R.F.a. posted — & A. Battery. Report Enquiries re. H.Q. gun. Remval.	
	30"	—	ALL of all recruits as N.C.O under for fatigue man of no army. There to be nothing under any. 1 found immediately after a short tial Red can be Shoeters without orders to shirt. 45 remounts from ROMSEY 27 from STHREHAMPTON. Many cases of symptoms in Ken; totamuch, flury, trainimy, Inners under manik, oppermiter	
	31"	—	Red story up — Lot of bi Irmen	

WAR DIARY or INTELLIGENCE SUMMARY

(Erase heading not required.)

Place	Date	Hour	Summary of Events and Information	Remarks and references to Appendices
BULFORD Camp	Sept 1st to 3rd		Routine.	
	4th		Inspection (made thoroughly). Odd mounts for Qr. M. Sergeants — a very poor show. Mules girth; harness not fitted — worn anyhow...	
	6th		Lt. Richardson, Goodman, Lord — reported from course LARKHILL, 2nd Batty. went for a course. Inspected booths of A Battery.	
	7th		A.D.S. Walton, Rifle joined from Sick Leave. Inspected booths of B.	
	8th		Capt. Holmes joined from Tenerife, his Germany. It states food from not leave, fer rk away futting.	
	9th		Lieut. GM.S. joined to Instruction purposes. Shoeing is very bad and instruction nil — Rode On Q. Laden set on horse.	
	10th		Inspected booths of C & D. Drivery is an. inspect & other material from A.S.M. Crowhis from G.P.O. came to listen on Telephones. —	
	11th		Setting lines put up for ret of Brigade—	
	13th		Apptd L. Watson asst to Brigade ris Allen & An. Cdt. L. Waterman joined temp.	
	14th		Lt. Campbell joined for Sp.Res.	
	15th		Inspection parade of "B"gnd.S.& Regt. A great want of reliable tools. People it all very bad. —	

WAR DIARY
or
INTELLIGENCE SUMMARY
(Erase heading not required.)

Army Form C. 2118

Instructions regarding War Diaries and Intelligence Summaries are contained in F. S. Regs., Part II. and the Staff Manual respectively. Title Pages will be prepared in manuscript.

Place	Date	Hour	Summary of Events and Information	Remarks and references to Appendices
BULFORD	Sept. 18	—	Drawing out of Equipt and Camps, from Ordnance — Bd. Am. Col. & Bd. H. Qrs. nearly complete. Telephone Equipt got.	
	19th	—	Routine. Battery staff & officers went out for preliminary scheme to Sidbury. Presence of Bulls in material.	
	20th	—	Routine. 2 K.H.O. & 5 men.	
	21st	—	Sent out Musketry at Batty — Rally gun drill "C", min range officers aftern. Cadres service lecture to commence tomorrow. Am: Col.	
	22nd	—	Battery from mill. Dummy drill sights.	
	23rd	—	3 to Apres on S.I. — D battery out as a battery. Col. Louis Tremance — Am. Col. to send majority of men.	
	24th	—	Leave for all ranks tomorrow.	
	25th	—	Scheme for Battery Staff & officers in afternoon.	
	26th	—	Remount of officers instructed, horses for transfer to R. Sqr. — A.S.C. Entrain by Rry.	
	27th	—	Very cold weather — horse rug will be required shortly. Entrain by Rry. maj.	
	28th	—	Maj. Gen Drake Y.g. Cd's inspected Brigade. 2 Batteries on Field. 2 in Barracks at Bath. Gun drill. Very well all officers evening — shew at Barrack, Artillery staff — guards etc.	
	29th	—	Artillery Gun drill. 2 batteries.	
	30th	—	It Anthews all day trekking at S.P. Drill — Empcy, Ladies etc It is impossible to prepare to fight work till the B.q.d. exact is done, absence of Maj. Gen.	

1875 Wt. W593/826 1,000,600 4/15 J.B.C. & A. A.D.S.S./Forms/C. 2118.

WAR DIARY
or
INTELLIGENCE SUMMARY

(Erase heading not required.)

Army Form C. 2118

Place	Date	Hour	Summary of Events and Information	Remarks and references to Appendices
Byford	Oct 1st	—	Pay Parade & 2 Lectures — In field — 15 Horses transferred to the Reg. Cav. Depot	
	2nd	—	Routine — wet — preparing scheme for next day —	
	3rd	—	Wet. — Scheme for Officers — Stable work —	
	4th	—	Scheme at 9 am - Drill — Officers schemes - much organic paper A.C.I. too	
			much to peruse properly — Conference with G.O.C. making out scheme & men for	
			Sun. + Mon. Time for lectures before Courses.	
	12 "		Routine	
	12"	—	1st Tactical Day with Brigade complete - want of knowledge not noticing we any movements	
			much dissipline lost. Turn out so good. Capt W.P. Kennett R.G.R. posted to "C" Batty.	
	14 "	—	2nd Brigade Day — much dissipline improving — let very much get to hand left in	
			flat — turn out a is best ready — reconnaissance etc — G.O.C. came out. —	
	16 "	—	3rd Brig. Day — a short Day — improvement is clear — much get to hand — want of instruments	
			sights, directors, glasses etc very much felt. Driving is still bad	
			[signature] Redwood Jones, Lt. Col.	

WAR DIARY or INTELLIGENCE SUMMARY

Army Form C. 2118

Place	Date	Hour	Summary of Events and Information	Remarks and references to Appendices
Bulford	July 17	—	At LONGSTOCK preparing scheme & marking bivouacs for Bde work. 2nd Lieut. into to 148-M R.G.A. — 2nd Lieut. J.S. Campbell joined on Staff from "R" R.M.A.	
	18			
	19			
	20			
	21		Brigade marched to LONGSTOCK for 3 days in bivouac. Batteries independently on actual scheme. All arrived very late & stopped any further work that day. M. Staff & County not all in till 10 p.m.	
	22		Tactical day. On ground near LONGSTOCK. G.O.C. came & inspected camps in aftn. Brigade operations failed owing to communications not being properly installed.	
	23		Brigade clear'd bivouac & marched back to BULFORD during morning. A good test, but much to be noted & corrected — no serious defects. Some late arrivals. —	
	24		Heavy rain all day. Drilling layed at Larkhill all day — Sn'g. Hunn Campbell joined from R.N.D. He not yet posted.	
	25		V. wet & cold wind. 2Lieut Moody & Osborne joined.	

Army Form C. 2118

WAR DIARY
or
INTELLIGENCE SUMMARY

(Erase heading not required.)

Instructions regarding War Diaries and Intelligence Summaries are contained in F. S. Regs., Part II. and the Staff Manual respectively. Title Pages will be prepared in manuscript.

Place	Date	Hour	Summary of Events and Information	Remarks and references to Appendices
Poulton Camp	Oct. 27			
	28			
	29		2nd Corp & Ostrere transferred to 162nd yds. Lieut. N.C. Coy R.F.A. joined to "C" Battery.	
	30			
	31			
	Nov 1st	—	Capt. Beckworth R.F.A. — Capt. H.A.T. Boulton R.F.A. joined units & Ammunition	
	2	—	"B" & "D" Batteries respectively. Lt. J.P. Knowles, S. Harris, J.E. Kagawin joined as 1st appts from R.M.A. —	
	3			
	4			

WAR DIARY or INTELLIGENCE SUMMARY

Army Form C. 2118

Place	Date	Hour	Summary of Events and Information	Remarks and references to Appendices
Bulford Camp	5			
	6		Orders received tonight to clear all accounts, preparatory to embarkation. Removal injunction detail of Officers & men to go with Brigade being prepared. 9 horses the seft —	
	7		Issue of stationery & other stores to complete. —	
	8		Very wet & stormy — Lecture by Brig. General Mess meeting of Brigade Officers — Col. W. Fall Arrival. Am Cal. in preparation for muster of Officers routine at Gun Drill Carpy rifle.	
	9			
	10			
	11			
	12		1st Gun practice – A Battery & Staff got out, after an hour's wait in the rain. Practice cancelled till it cleared & heavier gales & rain. Target invisible Shifts stages are ahead to 15 & 9 inr. no practice —	
	13		Ahad M wind clean. Rt Bing practice disappointing – very cold – Brig Gen't speech Staff over. Command of Brig —	
	14		Hoar frost – fine – 2nd Bing practice – not very satisfactory —	
	15		Frost —	
	16			
	17		Hoar frost – last day's practice – hit made all satisfactory – Drill works. Keen before big carrying attempt for this —	

WAR DIARY
or
INTELLIGENCE SUMMARY

(Erase heading not required.)

Army Form C. 2118

Place	Date	Hour	Summary of Events and Information	Remarks and references to Appendices
Bulford Camp	Nov 18th	—	Gun Drill – begin – Inspection Am. Col. by Genl. R.A. not good – 2Lt Turner to 2A. Res. Brigade –	
	19	—		
	23	—	Brig de Off[?] new accounts closed, blame held to O.R.[?] Nothorne in hopes but closing Sgt now seconded to home army	
	24	—		
	25	—	Reg'l S.A.A. horses gone from 166-18.85 – a 450 [?] gunners to B.S.M. – reports his mut -	
	26	—	a.R.S.m. hanny ahr to wel to B.S.M. – reports his mut. 30 men gun Inspection of Brigade in F.S. order at 11. a.m. by mute. 30 men gun Repair to Rn Roy Woolwich –	
	29	—	Br gone from	
	30	—	Reg't S. A. A. had gone from 166- Brigade Rifle – Again Am 2 Sgt they dead – Volume of £38-7.3. Indy of between M.C.A. Lt & Aug. Staff. – Completion of much[?] begun on H. range. – to be on every day.	
Dec.	1st 2d 6th	—	L/Sr. J.A. Campbell + W/Schunk proceeds to cause Telephony & Greatzette	
	7th	—	Asked second to precedl overseas on 11/6/12[?]th – Lr/Sr. J. Campbell recalled L/Sr. J. Sm Campbell preceded overseas in advance of Divn. –	

WAR DIARY / INTELLIGENCE SUMMARY

Army Form C. 2118

Place	Date	Hour	Summary of Events and Information	Remarks and references to Appendices
Bulford	8	—	Preparation for departure	
	9	—	Do — Am. Pickles issued	
	10	—	Do	
	11	—	Do — Army records etc.	
	12	—	—	
			Commenced entraining for SOUTHAMPTON at 4.30 a.m. Last train left at 3.25 p.m. Loading good — smooth — all hands up to time. Much delay experienced at Port owing to 2 ships being in wrong berth — 1 ship's Angles (berthing gear) trough had to be disembarked & shipped up amongst any available transport.	
	13		A. Qrs arrived at 4 a.m. at HAVRE but only details of Batteries till 1 a.m. On landing, it was found that only details of Batteries had arrived, so it was impossible to entrain as ordered, the 167 Bde Transports were therefore taken over by 166 Bde and the former Bde went into Rest Camp to await the rest of Batteries.	
	14		Remainder of Brigade arrived during night & went into Rest Camp. Brigade left for front H'Qrs & A. Battery entraining at 6.30 p.m.	
	15		Brigade arrived as follows: H'Qrs & A. Battery at THIENNE at 5.50 p.m. in billets 10.30 p.m.	
	16			

WAR DIARY or INTELLIGENCE SUMMARY

Army Form C. 2118

Place	Date	Hour	Summary of Events and Information	Remarks and references to Appendices
	16"		All batteries in billets by 5.30 pm. —	
	17"			
BERGUETTE	18"		C.O. proceeded to 2nd Div. Art. HQrs. at 10.30. Brig. W.C. Kennedy remained in command. 8 Officers & 39 men attached to 2nd Div. Arty. for training in 1st line. —	
	19"		20,80 rounds "gunfire". Drawn from B.A.C. — fine. —	
	20"		Completed drawing ammn. — weather very wet, roads f.c.	
	22"		C.O. & attached Officers + men to training (returned). Another batch (proceeded) to the front line. Brig. Genl. French, comdg. Corps arty. came to inspect with B.G. Comdg. Div. Arty.	
	23"		weather changeable. began drawing hay for horse standings —	
	24"		water in myth & miles — Am. Col. filled getting flooded —	
	25"		roads in myth. & Am. Col. under water — they were flooded up during day & dug of village.	
	26"		routine — working at billets — got 2 in oft. Sent round billets — 3rd detact. to 2nd Bel. returned. 2nd 3rd dets. —	
	27"		holy ground, 3 batteries went marching. —	

WAR DIARY
or
INTELLIGENCE SUMMARY

(Erase heading not required.)

Army Form C. 2118

19.

Place	Date	Hour	Summary of Events and Information	Remarks and references to Appendices
BERGUETTE	29th	—	Lt. Walthew arrived from front to hand over Ammunity Park. 2/Lt. Haycock attached to S.A.C. Lieut H.C. Cory appointed Capt. vice Walton to C Battery.	
"	30th	—	"C" Battery marched for front line – to be attached to Corps. Heavy Artillery at 10. am. 1 Subsection B.A.C. under Lieut. Waterman accompanied it – a detachment of D.A. Col. to join up at repair line.	
"	31st	—	Ground drying up, but road not in again in afternoon. Cable not yet ready much used.	

Dec 31st 1915

S/P Arthur Lay Lt Col
Comdg 167 Bde

Army Form C. 2118

WAR DIARY
or
INTELLIGENCE SUMMARY
(Erase heading not required.)

167 Brigade RFA

JAN^RY 1916

Sep - 1916

Place	Date	Hour	Summary of Events and Information	Remarks and references to Appendices
BERGUETTE	1st Jany		Lt Gordon A.V.C. joined.	
	2nd		Commenced returning shell boxes to Railhead along with ord. Stores came in. Day another few Blanket carrying on Brigade - end of actions were the day.	
	3rd		Finis.	
	6th		Brigade route march - Division reporting on battery positions. Lt Godm OCC offer in Temp Staff	
	7th		SltCay proceeded to Kitser B, section. Ard ance last half returned.	
	8th		[struck through]	
	9th		Brigade route marcht. D Battery marched with Brigade Stff. Lt Cay returned from detached pst	
	12th		Brigade Left yard from 6" gun - Lt Godm AVC rejoined from Ony.	
	13th		Your Left. yard front to ? Staff turn. Sick.	
	14		Very fine - half fine & frost at night. Staff turn. Sick.	
			with QMQ.	
	18th		Reconnaissance scheme for Brigade.	
	19th		GOC RA Corps rode round. Artillery Ellett - chin of Telephony started - which he worked in Reptery.	
	21st		Brigade route march - windy.	
	22nd		Inf using half to fire - OCC'O's. Supply & gun joined from No 2 Amm Sechcln.	
	23rd		Gun half & burbr, a fini day. "Stand by" order at night only struck at 2 hrs notice.	
	26th		Inspection by GOC.2C Corps.	
	27th		LC Dunfield (Maj) posted to Brd Arty my SCC Morgan who was transferred	
	28th		Brigade (less C/167) on manoeuvres with 12th Division. Brigade billeted at CRECHES	
	30th		for the night	
	31st		Manoeuvres finish. "Lieut V.W. Curtis joins the Brigade.	

McCoy Lieut RFA
Adjt 167 Bde
for O.C.

Army Form C. 2118

WAR DIARY
or
INTELLIGENCE SUMMARY.
(Erase heading not required.)

167 Brigade RFA

Instructions regarding War Diaries and Intelligence Summaries are contained in F. S. Regs., Part II. and the Staff Manual respectively. Title Pages will be prepared in manuscript.

Place	Date	Hour	Summary of Events and Information	Remarks and references to Appendices
BERGUETTE	1st Feb	—	D Battery and 1 section C Battery proceed to front to take over gun positions (only) of 47th Battery RFA, in action at LE MARAIS near GORRE. Lieut Sir J Campbell to RA HQ to understudy Staff Captain.	
	5	—	Lieut Sir J Campbell to 2nd Division. Aeroplane reported for C Battery, in action near CUINCHY, whilst doing Counter Battery work.	
	7	—	D Battery and 1 sect of B Bty return from their instruction at the front. A and 1 sect of C Batteries proceed to take over the position of 56th Battery for instruction. 2 Lieut E Morris and 2 Lieut J Campbell attached to Batteries in action for instruction.	
	9	—	C Battery receives instructions to move position to VERMELLES	
	11	—	These instructions are cancelled.	
	12	—	A number of 77 mm shell very near C Battery's position, no damage. 2 Lieut E Morris returns from front to take up duties of Orderly Officer.	
	13	—	A Battery and 1 sect of B Battery and Lieut J Campbell return from front.	
	14	—	B Battery and 1 subsection of the Ammunition Column permanently leave the Brigade and are posted to 1/4 London Brigade T.F.	
	15	—	Lt Col Harper proceeds to front to study the line.	
	16	—	Big gale, which blew down many tarpaulins over horse standings.	
	17	10 pm	B/c ordered to be ready to move at short notice.	
	18	midnight	" no longer to be " "	
			Lt Col Harper returns	
	19		Lieut Cory to BETHUNE to study the front. BETHUNE bombed for about one hour between 10 and 11 pm by hostile aircraft.	

Army Form C. 2118

167 Brigade RFA

WAR DIARY
or
INTELLIGENCE SUMMARY
(Erase heading not required.)

Instructions regarding War Diaries and Intelligence Summaries are contained in F. S. Regs., Part II. and the Staff Manual respectively. Title Pages will be prepared in manuscript.

Place	Date	Hour	Summary of Events and Information	Remarks and references to Appendices
AERGUETTE	20	11 am	Aeroplane again drops a bomb on BETHUNE. About 22 of our aircraft front DON. All return.	
	23		C Battery lets to stand by for Gas Alarm. This turns out to be smoke sent over towards GIVENCHY.	
			Left section of A Battery proceed to take over the position and wagon line of D/65 on the TOURBIERE LOOP (CAMBRIN)	
			Right section D Battery take over from B/65 in action near ANNEQUIN.	
		10 pm	C Battery ordered to move to wagon line	
	24			
	25	2 am	C Battery march to LE QUESNOY.	
			Remainder of A and D Batteries come into action. Right Section of C Battery makes a six gun battery with D Bty. Lt Section C Battery does ditto with A battery. Some of the men brought up in Motor omnibuses. Brigade HQ comes into action and take up their position North of ANNEQUIN relieving 64th Bde.	
	25–29		Stunt in registering. A certain amount retaliation for MINNENWERFER was done. New wires are laid and old system thoroughly overhauled.	

ACCoy Lieut RFA
Adjt 167 Bde RFA
for O.C.

WAR DIARY

167 (HOW) Brigade RFA

Army Form C. 2118

INTELLIGENCE SUMMARY

(Erase heading not required.)

References 1/40,000 BETHUNE. COMB. Sheet

Place	Date March	Hour	Summary of Events and Information	Remarks and references to Appendices
ANNEQUIN	1st		Bad weather. Batteries continue to register.	
	3rd		Snow. Bombardment of German trenches on our right by 12th Division. Two mines were exploded by us in an attempt to capture the salients of HOHENZOLLERN REDOUBT, known as "Big and Little Willie". This was partially successful. Bombing and shelling on both sides continued throughout the night.	
		9.30p	A Battery fired 51 rounds on CORONS DE MARON (A.29.C.) at intervals to help the 12th Division.	
	4th		D and E Battery co-operated in bombardment by 12th Div by firing on crater near HOHENZOLLERN REDOUBT and MADAGASCAR HOUSES. Observation impossible owing to snow-rain. A Bty retaliated for hostile MINENWERFER. PONT FIXE shelled by 5.9". Enemy attempted to retake craters lost day before but the attempt failed.	
	5th		MINENWERFER fired on BRICKSTACKS. D Bty retaliated for another MINENWERFER fire near MINE POINT.	
		noon till 4pm	15cm Hows shelled one of our 60 pr Batteries near Brigade H.Q. Very fine shooting but remarkably little damage done. Lt Col E.A. HARPER ceased to 33rd C.C. Station BETHUNE and Col ROCHFORT BOYD took command of "A" group.	
		10 pm	Test gas Alarm. First battery fired 10 secs after receipt of order.	
	6th		D & E Bty made a direct hit on a suspected hostile observing station. Causing a fire for 15 mins.	
		11.15p	A & C Bty made some direct hits on a hostile working party at A.16.a.7.4½. and a gun fired on CORONS DE MARONS (23 rounds). Germans did a lot of work during this day.	

WAR DIARY

Army Form C. 2118

167 (How) Brigade RFA

INTELLIGENCE SUMMARY

References 40,000 BETHUNE COMB: Sheet

Place	Date	Hour	Summary of Events and Information	Remarks and references to Appendices
ANNEQUIN	6th (Contd)		Orders received that 167 Brigade HQ will go out of action on 8th	
	7th		B'th Amn Column moved nearer the front to billets in BETHUNE (E.5.D.2.2). Very bad weather for observing. A & C Bty fired on area A.22.A.3.2 - A.22.A.2.3 in conjunction with the blowing up of a mine by our infantry just N of LA BASSÉE ROAD and also retaliated for hostile MINENWERFER fire. PRINGLE, Adjt 156 Bde RFA, comes to A Group HQ to take over from Lieut. Re Cory, Adjt. 167 Bde RFA.	
	8th	6.15 pm	A & C Bty fired on CORONS DE MARONS in conjunction with activity on that front. Both Batteries as usual retaliated for hostile MINENWERFER fire. 167 Bde. H.Q. move in to BETHUNE and 156 Bde HQ move into their place. 2/Lt EMORRIS, Orderly Officer 167 Bde, remains to hand over L⁄Cpl HARPUR evacuated to BASE	
	9th		A & B Bty fired 55 rounds in salvoes in retaliation for shelling of our BRICKSTACKS by 15 cm HOW. Also fired on hostile front trenches North of CANAL in conjunction with mine exploded at GIVENCHY. D & C Bty fired on a medium gun emplacement in MADAGASCAR trench. Several direct hits were obtd.	
	12th		Both Batteries fired about 20 rounds. This was about average for a quiet day during this time	
	13th		Both Batteries retaliated for MINENWERFER	
	14th 15th		A + C fired 73 Rounds in retaliation for MINENWERFER firing near LA BASSÉE RD. This weapon has been very active recently this month and Infantry continually called for retaliation, as its moral effect is so great	

WAR DIARY
INTELLIGENCE SUMMARY

167 (How) Brigade RFA Army Form C. 2118

(Erase heading not required.)

Place	Date	Hour	Summary of Events and Information	Remarks and references to Appendices
	17th		A & ½ C Battery stopped the Aerial Torpedo firing with 9 rounds. Ammunition ration cut to 4 rounds a gun per diem.	
	18th	5.45 pm to 7.45 pm	Both batteries fired in conjunction with a hostile attack in the craters near the HOHENZOLLERN REDOUBT. The enemy bombarded promiscuously with lachrymatory shell; most batteries and HQ "wept". Including our own Batteries. Wagons lines near BEUVRY even filled it. Gases pm at 7.45 pm	
	23rd	11 pm	Test gas alarm.	
	26th		D & ½ C Battery moved to their new gun pits in the houses near ANNEQUIN.	
	27th		A & ½ C " fired 57 rounds at BRICKSTACK area in retaliation for the hy MINENWERFER.	
	29th		D & ½ C Battery dispersed a working party near INDIAN WELL HOUSE.	
	31st		Bombing attack by our infantry near A BRICKSTACK at night. A & ½ C Bty fired 120 rounds at area D-M. BRICKSTACKS.	

M.C.Cory. LIEUT.
ADJUTANT 167TH (HOWITZER) BDE. R.F.A.

Army Form C. 2118

XXXIII / 167 Brigade RFA Vol 3

WAR DIARY
or
INTELLIGENCE SUMMARY

167 Brigade RFA

(Erase heading not required.)

Place	Date	Hour	Summary of Events and Information	Remarks and references to Appendices
	APRIL			
	1st		A + ½ C still in action at CAMBRIN D + ½ C at ANNEQUIN (SOUTH) B & H.Q still in rest at BETHUNE.	
	3rd		2 officers + 30 men from 186 Bde RFA attached to D/167 for instruction	
	9th		" " " " " " " " " left	
	20th		Enemy fired at Fosse No 9 with 8 inch. F,G,H,K,L,M BRICKSTACKS were fired at by A + ½ C/167 in conjunction with infantry raid. About 50 rounds were fired by D/167 for registration under direction of Aeroplane observer.	
	21st			
	27th		Gas Attack to our right which was felt near Battery positions and as far back as BETHUNE. At the batteries you could hardly see your finger in front of your face.	
	28th		Curious incident near A/167. Hostile aeroplane dropped a circular saying that they had a certain house was an advanced dressing station but they would have to shell it as a howitzer battery was close behind it, which did great damage.	
	29th		Enemy shelled HARLEY STREET and demolished the advanced dressing station mentioned.	

M℃ory Lieut. RFA
Cdg 167 Bde RFA

Reference Map Sheet
36 N.W.1. 1/10000 XXXIII

MAY
Army Form C. 2118

167 Brigade RFA. Vol 4

WAR DIARY
or
INTELLIGENCE SUMMARY
(Erase heading not required.)

Place	Date MAY	Hour	Summary of Events and Information	Remarks and references to Appendices
In the Field	11th		Enemy sprung a mine near HOHENZOLLERN REDOUBT, followed by a strong infantry attack, about 36 hr front line for about 500 yds was held. B Battery (from D/162) fired 237 rounds on MAD ALLEY A.28.D. (Mutual Support Scheme). A Battery (from D/156) was first in support of 15th Division. 2 Lieut N S BOSTOCK attached to B Battery posted to C Battery 162 Brigade.	
	10th		A Battery fired in support of said by 16th R.R's.	
	15th			
	20th		Re-organisation of 33rd Divnl Artillery 167 Brigade (Hows) now composed of following Batteries. D Battery. 156 Bde., D Bty 162 Bde, D Bty 166 Bde. The old Batteries were disposed of as follows:- A Battery became D/156, C Battery became D/162, D Battery became A/166 Bd	
	22nd		A Battery relieved by C/166 and left BETHUNE at 11 pm for MAZINGHEM for training at 11th Corps Artillery Training School. A Battery returned from training and C Battery who went out for training	
	31st		During this period A Battery was in action at from 1st to 22nd at CUINCHY STATION (1 section only) doing duty as enfilade section of AUCHY Group and enfilading trenches - RAILWAY, MADAGASCAR and FOSSE No 8 (A.27, 28, 29). The then section was attached to B/156 at F.18.A.32.
C Battery was in CUINCHY Group and in action at F.24.A.3.9 and shooting on trenches South of LARASSÉE - BETHUNE ROAD.
B Battery was in action in VERMELLES and was in AUCHY Group. This battery occupied the most southern position of the 33rd Divisional Artillery

J.F.Cory Lieut/Act. RFA
OC 167 Brigade RFA | |

Army Form C. 2118

WAR DIARY
or
INTELLIGENCE SUMMARY
(Erase heading not required.)

167th Brigade A.F.A.

Instructions regarding War Diaries and Intelligence Summaries are contained in F.S. Regs., Part II. and the Staff Manual respectively. Title Pages will be prepared in manuscript.

Place	Date JUNE	Hour	Summary of Events and Information	Remarks and references to Appendices
France.	1/6/16		A Bty relieved C/Bty at ANNEQUIN N. C/Bty proceeded to MAZINGHEM for training	
	11/6/16		A Bty was relieved by C Bty who came again into action at ANNEQUIN N.	
	13/6/16		1 Sect of A Bty relieved 1 sect of a battery 38th Div. at LAVENTIE	
	16/6/16		1 Sect of A Bty returned to wagon lines at BETHUNE from LAVENTIE	
	17/6/16		A Bty took over from B/174 39th Div and came into action N of LA BASSÉE CANAL at A/3.B.	
	24/6/16-30/5/16		A B & C Batteries carried out wire cutting operations	Appendix 1 (copy only)
	27/28		(B Battery took part in raid) See Appendix	
			HOSTILE ACTIVITY	
			Enemy sprung several mines on our front and occasionally bombarded our communication & support trenches.	
			OPERATIONS.	
			Nothing of importance to report. Batteries occupied in wire cutting, dispersing hostile working parties and putting up barrages for mining operations.	
Battery Positions:			A Bty N of LA BASSÉE CANAL at A/3.B. B Bty at VERMELLES. C Bty at ANNEQUIN NORTH.	

McCoy Lieut Maj
for Lieut Col
Comdg 167 Bde R.F.A.

Army Form C. 2118

33 JUNE
VOL 5

167th Brigade R.F.A.

WAR DIARY
or
INTELLIGENCE SUMMARY
(Erase heading not required.)

Instructions regarding War Diaries and Intelligence Summaries are contained in F. S. Regs., Part II. and the Staff Manual respectively. Title Pages will be prepared in manuscript.

Place	Date JUNE	Hour	Summary of Events and Information	Remarks and references to Appendices
France	1/6/16		A Bty relieved C Bty at ANNEQUIN N. C Bty proceeded to MAZINGHEM for training	
	11/6/16		A Bty was relieved by C Bty who came into action at ANNEQUIN N.	
	13/6/16		1 sect of A Bty relieved 1 sect of a battery 38th Bde at LAVENTIE	
	14/6/16		1 sect of A Bty returned to wagon lines at BETHUNE from LAVENTIE	
	17/6/16		A Bty took over from B/174 39th Div and came into action N/of LA BASSÉE CANAL at A13.B.	
	24/6/16 30/5/16		A B & C Batteries carried out wire cutting operations	
			## HOSTILE ACTIVITY	
			Enemy opened several minor our own front and occasionally bombarded our communication & support trenches.	
			## OPERATIONS	
			Nothing of importance to report. Batteries occupied in wire cutting, dispersing working parties and putting up barrages for minor operations.	
Battery Positions			A Bty N of LA BASSEE CANAL at A13.B. B Bty at VERMELLES. C Bty at ANNEQUIN NORTH.	

McBey Lieut Artyt
for Lieut Col
Comdg 167 Bde RFA

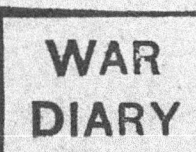

Headquarters,

167th BRIGADE, R.F.A.

(33rd Division)

J U L Y

1 9 1 6

Attached:

Appendices I, II, III, IIIa & IV.

Reference Map Sheet 33 of Fr⟨ance⟩

MONTAUBAN + MARTIN PUICH

167. Brigade R.F.A. Vol 6

Army Form C. 2118

WAR DIARY or INTELLIGENCE SUMMARY

(Erase heading not required.)

Instructions regarding War Diaries and Intelligence Summaries are contained in F.S. Regs., Part II. and the Staff Manual respectively. Title Pages will be prepared in manuscript.

Place	Date JULY	Hour	Summary of Events and Information	Remarks and references to Appendices
CUINCHY SECTOR	5th	6 pm	Received orders that Seaforth Artillery would be relieved. 1 Section of C/167 moves to their wagon lines.	
	6th	dusk	Their wagon lines from position at ANNEQUIN. NORTH A and B and 1 section of C Battery moved out to their wagon lines.	
	7th	6 pm	HQ relieved by a Bde HQ of 39th Division. The whole Brigade then proceeded to village of L'ECLEME, near BUSNES	
	10th	1pm 3am	Brigade entrained at CHOCQUES, and entrained at LONGEAU at about 9 am and 11 am. Bde marched in two columns to LE MESGE via AMIENS - AILLY - PICQUIGNY.	
	12th	9 am	arriving about 4 pm and 7 pm. 11am Received orders to stand ready to move. Marched out at 3 pm, proceeding Battery Drill orders. Received orders to stand ready to move. Marched out at 3 pm, proceeding via AMIENS to VECQUEMONT where Bde billeted in same village as 166 and 162 Brigades 156 Bde was billeted at CORBIE.	
	13th	8 am	Marched out and arrived at MARRET-WOOD near TREUX at 12 noon. Here the Bde bivouached in the wood	
	14th	1 am	Received warning orders to move. Marched out at 3 am. and Whole Divnl Artillery moved together via MEAULTE. 167 Bde halted at BECORDEL-BECOURT at 5.30 am Marched again at 2 pm Roads very congested. Halted on top of a hill on way. left of main road about 800 yds W. of FRICOURT. 167 Bde moved into valley below for night. During the night about 40 gas shells fell round the lines but no harm done	
	15th	4.30 am	Started out to reconnoitre Battery Positions near MAMETZ WOOD. Bde moved off at 10 am and marched to a position of assembly at about S. 30. B. 5.5. Great difficulty in getting there owing to number of battery shooting. HQ taken up in	
	16th	3 pm	German gun position at S. 25. A. 4.8. B + C Battys later took up positions at about S. 20. B. 8.7 North of CATERPILLAR WOOD. A Battery came into position about 7 pm in same place. Bde close together in line. Regd SWITCH TRENCH 5½ S.R.1 in front of O.P.	

1875 Wt. W593/826 1,000,000 4/15 J.B.C. & A. A.D.S.S./Forms/C.2118.

Army Form C 2118

WAR DIARY or INTELLIGENCE SUMMARY

167 Brigade R.F.A.

(Erase heading not required.)

Place	Date	Hour	Summary of Events and Information	Remarks and references to Appendices
	July 17		Zones of Batteries were as follows:- A Battery S.2.B.6.7 — S.2.B.9.9. B " Road S.2.B.25.55 — S.2.B.6.7 C " S.2.A.94 — S.2.B.25.55.	
	18		2,000 rounds per Bde any how were fired during the day on their zones. Heavy shelling by enemy 2 hrs NC FOR BEL and JUNCT CHAP north and South BAZENTIN to A and C Batteries respectively. Bombardment and attack on HIGH WOOD from 7pm to 10pm fort further reports.	
	19th		2.O.R. wounded. Battery positions shelled with shrapnel most of the day. Ridge in front heavily shelled with 8 inch all day. 2 O.R. wounded.	
	20th	2.65 AM	Batteries commence to shell HIGH WOOD at rate of 1 round a gun a minute	See Appendix II
		3.25 AM	Infantry assault HIGH WOOD.	
		9 am	Communication from Battery Positions forward cut. Received news from Forward Observing Officer C. Battery that our infantry had gained their objective and held the wood.	
		12.30pm 6 pm	Italian Counter attack made. Enemy's barrage very heavy. Received information that our infantry still held Southern portion of HIGH WOOD, but casualties very heavy.	
		9.30pm	Enemy forms heavy Gas shell barrage near Ridge. Shelling heavy. Batteries increased rate of fire to one round a gun a minute.	
	about 21st	11 pm	Enemy counter attack delivered. Situation quieter about 2 am. Reports received that our infantry had fallen back to original line in front of BAZENTIN-LE-PETIT WOOD	
		8 am	This report proves false as a new report shows that we still held of HIGH WOOD.	
		11 am	Enemy shelled road near Htrp 15 le with 15 cm.	

WAR DIARY or INTELLIGENCE SUMMARY

Army Form C. 2118

167. Brigade R.F.A.

Date	Hour	Summary of Events and Information	Remarks and references to Appendices
JULY 21	1 am	Battery shelled with 10.5 and 15 cm. Direct hit on B Battery telephone dugout. Casualties 3 killed (including B.S.M.), 5 wounded. One telephonist of C Battery also missing from 20th. Last seen laying wire to HIGH WOOD.	
	10.15 pm	Bombardment on right of our front commenced. Apparently a hostile counter attack as enemy fired heavy barrage and fired Lachrymatory and poisonous gas shells round CATERPILLAR WOOD. All wires cut again. Lamp station worked well in spite of flashes in the sky.	
	11 pm	All quiet again	
22nd		Heavy firing broke out at 2 pm, 3.30 pm, 4.30 pm or near Bar up and so on. R.S.M. and a Driver wounded coming up Horse killed.	See Appendix II
	5 p	Receive orders to bombard enemy night of 22/23rd	
	7 p	Bombardment commenced. Rate of fire 18 pm 20 rounds per gun per hour	
	8 p	Very heavy barrage from enemy fly away	
23rd	1.30 am	Attack commenced	
	3 am	Infantry attack held	
	5 am	Enemy counter attack. Fire of 18 pdr Bties turned on to SWITCH TRENCH and rate of fire increased to 1 round per gun per minute.	
	8.30 a	All afflied guns on our front.	
		Casualties 22nd, 23rd 6 wounded (including R.S.M.)	
24th 5.30 p		Enemy seen to be bringing up trenches.	
	6.45 p	Heavy hostile barrage opened. B Battery fire increased to 2 rounds per gun per minute. Bombardment on both sides very heavy.	
	10 p	Information received that counter attack broke down under our barrage. Rate of fire returned to normal. Casualties to day one wounded	

1875 Wt. W593/826 1,000,000 4/15 J.B.C. & A. A.D.S.S./Forms/C. 2118.

WAR DIARY or INTELLIGENCE SUMMARY

Army Form C. 2118

167 Brigade R.F.A.

Place	Date JULY	Hour	Summary of Events and Information	Remarks and references to Appendices
	25	12 noon	Heavy bombardment of trench area by enemy in nature of guns up to 12 inch from CATERPILLAR WOOD and North of MAMETZ WOOD from	
		4.30 p	to POMMIERS REDOUBT. Casualties 5 O.R. wounded	
		9 p	H.Q. B.gn. bombarded with gas shells	
	26	1 am	Bally zone altered as shown in Appendix	Appendix III
	27	7 am	Orders received for attack on LONGUEVAL and DELVILLE WOOD	
		6 pm	Bombardment orders received	
		5.30 pm	Bombardment commenced. Rates of fire, zones etc as shown in appendix	Appendix III A
		7.10 AM	Attack commenced	
		10 pm	Gas shell barrage fired in valley near H.Q. B.gde	
		6 am	Attack reported success on right but held up on left in LONGUEVAL VILLAGE. Casualties 2/Lt K.F.S. TURNER, A Battery, wounded. 2 O.R. wounded	
	28	12 noon	Barrage fired North of DELVILLE WOOD in cooperation with V th Div Infantry	
		10.30 pm	Heavy hostile bombardment. S.O.S. Signal sent up between HIGH WOOD and DELVILLE WOOD. Batteries fired 2 rounds per gun per minute	
		11.15 pm	All quiet - Counter attack reported to have petered away under our fire	
		11.30 pm	Heavy bombardment on our left. Casualties 2 O.R. wounded	
	29	6 am	Bombardment of SWITCH TRENCH SE of HIGH WOOD. 45 rounds per gun fired	
		3 pm	All C Battery's guns out of action. Battery return to wagon lines. Casualties 1 O.R. wounded	
		5.30 pm	Heavy shelling all along front. Batteries intense rate 2 rounds per gun per minute	

Army Form C. 2118

WAR DIARY
or
INTELLIGENCE SUMMARY   167 Brigade R.F.A.
(Erase heading not required.)

Place	Date	Hour	Summary of Events and Information	Remarks and references to Appendices
	JULY 30th	1pm to 5pm	Heavy shelling round battisan and Bde HQ. This seemed mainly directed against the road running past HQ. Casualties in wounds (O.R.)	Appendix IV
		6.10h	Our infantry attacked from HIGH WOOD to DELVILLE WOOD. Slight gun in ground but attack was held up on left and right.	
	31st		Shelling near Battery positions during night but little during the day. Capt. G. Fetherston C Battery slightly wounded, but remained at duty. 2 Lieut. FORBES badly wounded. One O.R. killed, one O.R. wounded. 2 guns of C Battery in action again	

J.C. ing Lieut. M.H.
for Lt. Col.
Comdg 167 Bde

7/5/16.

APPENDICES

I, II, III, IIIa & IV.

O.C. A B C /167   APPENDIX I

1) Bombardment commences at 2.55 AM at 3.25 am batteries lift to BLACK line. At 3.35 AM batteries lift to RED line and afterwards gradually back to final barrage line.

2) Rates of Fire

2.55 AM to 3.5 AM	1 round per gun per minute
3.5 AM to 3.25 AM	2 " " " "
3.25 AM to 3.35 AM	4 " " " "
3.35 AM to 3.55 AM	2 " " " "
3.55 AM to 4.25 AM	1 " " " " 2 mins
4.5 4.35.	See overleaf

After 4.25 AM fire will be maintained on final barrage line at the usual night firing rate.

During preliminary bombardment batteries will search HIGH WOOD up to RED line with a small percentage of their rounds. Mostly H.E. should be used on HIGH WOOD except on front edge of the wood and for 2 or 3 minutes before each lift.

O.C. C/167 will send a F.O.O. to S.q.A.O.5. to meet 1st CAMERONIANS with whom he will maintain liaison during the advance. He must be

(2) Rates of Fire.

2.55 am to 3.5 am   1 round per gun per min
3.5 am to 3.15 am   2   "   "   "   "
3.15 am to 3.25 am   4   "   "   "   "
3.25 am to 3.55 am   1   "   "   "   "
3.55 am to 4.25 am   1   "   "   "   2 "

accompanied by telephonists and sufficient telephone wire – He should proceed immediately.

Note. Re para ① 2nd line reads "batteries lift to BLACK line". This means no firing will take place on area this side of that line after the lift.

② Zones of Fire are as shown on attached Map, but batteries should be careful to overlap their fire a little.

night of 19/20th 12.45 pm

H.C.Coy. Lieut RFA
Adjt 167 Bde

New Zones will be taken over from the commencement of the bombardment

H.C.C.

… Bombardment Orders APPENDIX II

1. There will be a bombardment of SWITCH TRENCH and HIGH WOOD North of a line running from S.4.B.0.2 to S.3.D.95.80. commencing 7 pm and lasting till 12.30 am

2. At 12.30 am the Infantry will assault the trench and wood from S.5.A.0.5 to M.33.D.4.0.

3. The 3rd Corps will assault SWITCH TRENCH on our left.

4. The fire will be regular and should be on the trench and wood except that 18 prs should search ~~beyond~~ & back for 200 yards or 300 yards two or three times each hour.

5. At 12.30.am 18 prs will search back for 200 yards by short lifts and will continue ~~firing~~ to search the ground for 300 or 400 yards back at frequent intervals until no longer required

6. Ammunition Allowance
    18 prs – 20 rounds per gun per hour

7. Zones.
    33 Divnl Artillery
    from S.5.A.0.5 to S.4.A.4.4.

167-Brigade Orders   2.

1. ~~Guns~~ Zones will be as shown on attached map.
   Reference para 4 ~~batteries~~ Bombardment Orders, batteries when searching back will pay special attention to cross roads and road junctions as under.

   Battery.   Road junctions.
   A Battery   M.34.D.8.3.
   C Battery   { M.34.D.15.15.
                        { S.4.B.1.9.

2. Ammunition Allowance will be as shown in para 6 Bombardment Orders.
   Fire for the last 8 (eight) minutes before zero will be intense — 4 rounds per gun per minute.
   Shrapnel should be burst low so that any wire remaining will be cut.
   Proportion of ammunition will be 4 rounds of Shrapnel to 1 round of H.E.

3. "Zero" Time is 12.30 AM on the night of 22/23rd July
   This will only be communicated to those immediately concerned. No reference to it will be made on the telephone

   PTO   H Coy dr
                          A+H 167 Bde

APPENDIX III

A.B.C./167

Reference this office x 147 of 15th
instant para 2 Zones of Batteries
have now been altered as follows:-

A Battery   S.11.8.4.5. to S.5.D.00
B   S.5.D.00   to S.5.C.6.4.
C   S.5.C.6.4. to S.5.C.2.5.

Zones will all overlap a little on their
left and right

26/1/16   J Clay Lieut RFA
9 am   Adj // 13th Bde RFA

APPENDIX III A.166.

The 2nd and 5th Divns will attack and capture the remainder of LONGUEVAL village and DELVILLE WOOD.

The attack will be preceded by a bombardment commencing at 1 hour before Zero.

The attack will be carried out in the form of a methodical progression from point to point under cover of the artillery barrage.

The final line to be established by 5th Div will be — Orchard S.11.D. Central. — enclosure S.11.D.0.8. — thence approximately the line of the road running Westwards towards S.10.D.9.9.

Green flares will be used. Flares will be lit on the final line and also at 9 am and 2 pm.

2. 33rd D.A. Orders

162nd & 167th Bdes will search and sweep the whole of the area to be attacked North of Dark Olive Green line and West of Artillery dividing line as the various lifts take place

As the various lifts take place the Southern boundary for 33rd Div Arty will always be one lift in front of the area next to be attacked.
There will be no dividing line for 162nd and 167th Bdes. Both Brigades will cover the whole area.
Care must be taken not to fire too close to the Southern Edge next to be attacked.
When the final barrage is formed by 5th Divnl Arty, i.e. 2 Hours after Zero, 33rd Div Arty will resume their ordinary work and present zones except that they will search approaches more actively until new position has been consolidated.
The Hour of Zero will be 7.10 AM on July 27th. The bombardment will commence at 6.10 AM. These hours are on no account to be communicated by wire or telephone and only to those whom it is necessary to inform.
The fire will be intense for the last seven (7) minutes before each lift.
18prs will fire as large a proportion of HE as possible against the Wood and village.

167 Brigade Orders

1. Battery Zones will be as shown on Map P attached.

2. During bombardment there will be no fire South or West of Dash Olive Green Line.
   At Zero batteries will lift to RED Line
   At 1 hour after Zero (8.10 AM) batteries will lift to Green Line.
   At 1 hour 30 mins after Zero (8.40 AM) batteries will lift to Yellow line.
   At 2 hours after Zero (9.10 am) batteries will resume their ordinary work.

3. Rates of Fire
   1st Hour — 1½ rounds per gun per minute
   afterwards — 1 round per gun per minute
   The last seven (7) minutes before each lift will be intense = 3 rounds per gun per minute.

4. Ammunition
   As much H E as possible will be used when firing at DELVILLE WOOD and LONGUEVAL Village
   26/7/16 8 pm   Adjt 167 Bde

X 170

Ref. 53 DA BM/5/507
Operation orders for tomorrow 27th

Orders are amended as follows:

1. Bombardment will commence two hours before Zero. i.e. 5.10 AM

2. The brown (i.e. dark olive green line) will be omitted.

167th Bde barrage therefore begins at the Red line

at Zero batteries will lift to the Green line

at 1 Hour after Zero (8.10 AM) lift to Yellow line

at 1 hour 30 minutes after Zero (8.40 AM) batteries will resume their ordinary work and zones - except that they will search approaches more actively

Zero is 7.10 AM.
Remaining orders stand good

27/7 -16
12.20 am

L. M....
Lt 2 167 BdeRA

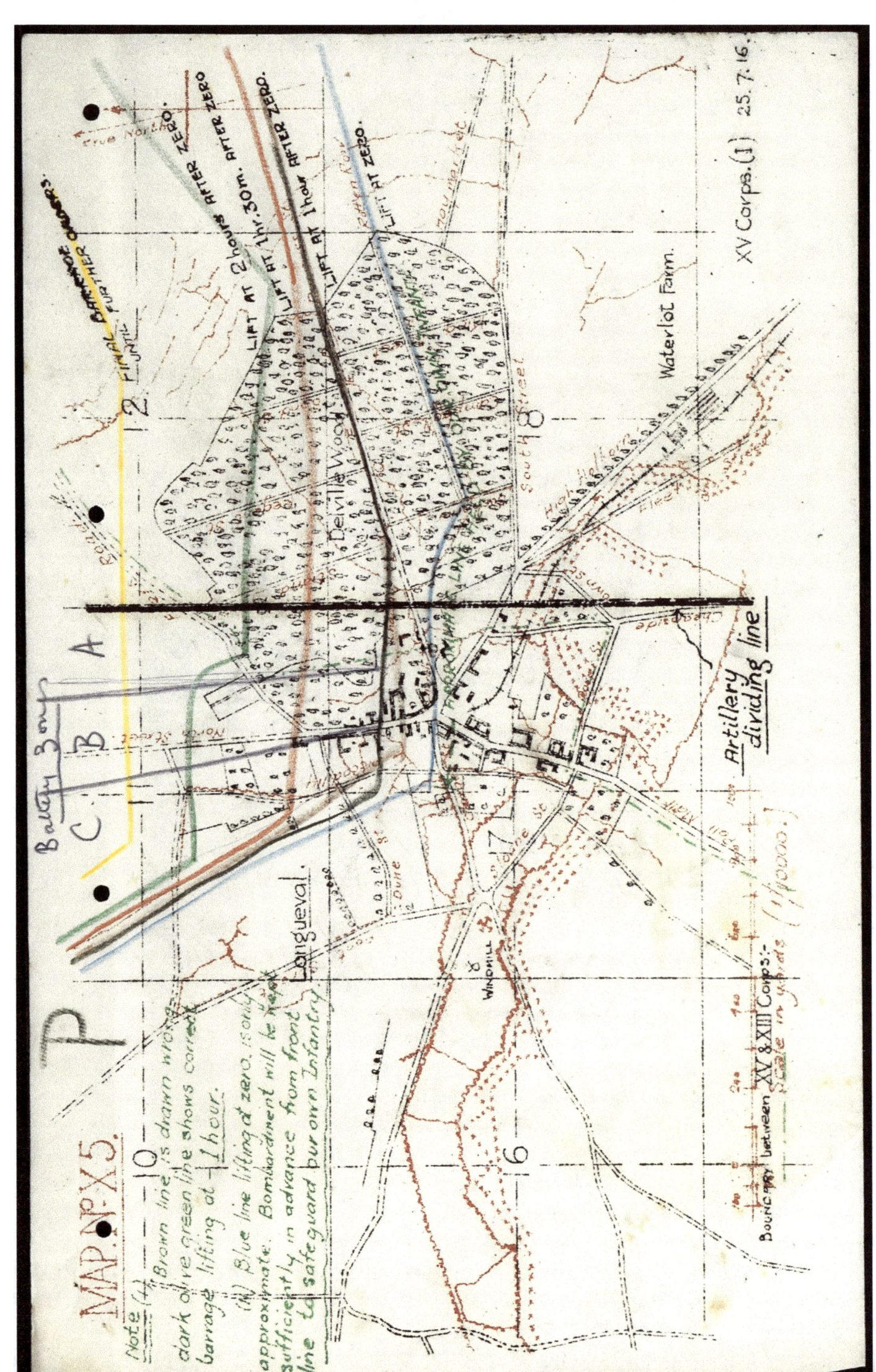

APPENDIX IV

1/7 -- oo M+L MARTINPUICH

1. An attack will be made on the German line running from S11D39 – S11D08 – S11C58 – North West to High Wood.

2. Zero will be at 6-10 pm on July 30th. No times are to be communicated on telephone.

3. The bombardment will commence at 4-45 pm. It will commence slowly and gradually quicken up, the last seven minutes being as intense as possible.

4. The 5th D.A. will bombard the trench to be attacked from S11D39 to S11D08 to S11C58 to S11A32.

5. Action of 33 R.A as on attached table.

6. The 51 D.A. will bombard the trench from S11A32 – S11B79 – S4D5C and the trench from that point to the East corner of High Wood.

7. The strongpoint at East corner of High Wood is being dealt with by Trench Mortars.

(2)

8. The Heavy Artillery will bombard the trenches from S.4.D.3.9. – S.4.D.0.6. – S.11.C.5.6. – S.10.B.9.9. – S.4.D.55.65 – thence to East corner of High Wood, but will not fire closer to High Wood than 100 yards. Heavy Artillery will also bombard Switch Trench between S.6.C.7.5 and N.33.D.5.0, and search the more distant approaches.

9. At Zero 18 pr will search back by lifts for 200 yards and will search the ground beyond at frequent intervals with the exception of 33 D.A. 18 pr. The 33 D.A. 18 pr will continue on their targets at the same rates for half an hour and then gradually slow down – stopping when no longer required.

10. Ammunition allotted from 4.45 pm to 6.40 pm
33 D.A. 18 pr -- 100 rounds per gun

11/7 Bde. Orders

1. Zones Barraging Switch Trench
   11.7 Bde Zone
      S.5.A.3.3. to S.5.D.3.9.
   Battery zones
   A Battery S.5.A.7.0 - S.5.D.3.9
   B   "   S.5.A.5.3 - S.5.A.7.0.
   C   "   S.5.A.3.3 - S.5.A.5.3.

2. Rates of Fire
   4.45 pm - 5.15 pm   1 round per gun per 2 mins
   5.15 pm - 5.50 pm   2   "   1   "
   5.50 pm - 6.3 pm   2   "   1   "
   6.3 pm - 6.10 pm   4   "   1   "
   6.10 pm - 6.25 pm   2   "   1   "
   6.25 pm - 6.40 pm   1   "   1   "
   and then slow down

3. Ammunition
      200 rounds per gun
      Proportion ½ A ½ AX

4. Switch Trench to be barraged and
   ground on North and South of it
   searched 300 yds short and 400 yds
   over

   30/7/16   A Clayton
   4.30 pm   Adjt 11/7 Bde

33rd Divisional Artillery

167th BRIGADE

ROYAL FIELD ARTILLERY

AUGUST 1916

Reference Map Sheets
MONTAUBAN
HARTINPUICH

Army Form C. 2118

WAR DIARY
or
INTELLIGENCE SUMMARY
(Erase heading not required.)

167 Brigade R.F.A.   Vol 7

Place	Date August	Hour	Summary of Events and Information	Remarks and references to Appendices
	1.	5h 30	Germany night firing heavy on the right (10 rds per Bde per hour) Heavy shelling near Bde HQ. Casualties nil.	
	2.	4 am	156th and 167th Bdes came under orders of 51st Div Arty who relieved 33rd Div Arty. Bde pone S.11.A.4.0 to S.16.A.0.7. Day firing as usual. Battery positions very heavily shelled all day from 10 am to about 4 pm.	
		5:30	A Battery fire on Bde zone at rate of 4 rounds per minute and searched back to 400 yards beyond trench. Casualties 3 O.R. killed 3 wounded. 3 O.R. wounded returned to duty.	
		7 pm		
	3		B Battery moves into taken up position at S.27.A.3.5 near Montauban village. Lt Col Lt Goff sick and went to hospital. Major D. Stewart took over command of the Bde.	
	4		C Battery again shelled and moved into position near B Battery. A Battery heavily shelled. One gun hit. 1 O.R. killed.	
	6		A Battery moves into position near B and C Batteries forming a six gun Battery. 33rd Div Infantry relieve 51st Div infantry in the trenches. Battery shelled during night. One team lost and 3 horses badly wounded.	
	9	evening	6 gun Bnt by 162 Bde to complete establishment of guns. 6 gun of the Brigade out of action owing to broken springs. Capt Talbot takes command of the six gun and moved into position in front of the other 6 gun Battery.	

Original
Army Form C. 2118

WAR DIARY
or
INTELLIGENCE SUMMARY 167 Brigade RFA

(Erase heading not required.)

Place	Date AUGUST	Hour	Summary of Events and Information	Remarks and references to Appendices
	10th		Capt. C.H. WALKER takes temporary command of B Battery.	
	11th	2 am	Orders received that Brigade would be relieved by 162nd Brigade on the night of 11th/12th.	
		6 pm	Batteries and HQ relieved.	
		6.15pm	Relief reported finished. Brigade billeted at DERNANCOURT. Short leave to PARIS granted to officers.	
	14th		Lt Col C G STEWART. C.M.G. D.S.O. took over command of the Brigade vice Major D. STEWART who returned to his battery. Lt Col L.T.G. OFF evacuated. (13/1/12)	
	15th		2/Lt E. M. HORNCASTLE evacuated.	
	17th		Lt. T.T. BOWMAN R.A.M.C. joined unit.	
	19th	5 am 12 noon	Ammunition (8 wagons each time) sent up to 162 Brigade.	
			2 Lieut G.T. STANLEY CLARK joined the Brigade and posted to B Battery. Capt. S. NOCKOLDS R.A.M.C. " " " vice Lt. BOWMAN R.A.M.C. Positions reconnoitred round FRICOURT for the Brigade in ease of having to reinforce the Artillery in the line.	
	22nd	5 pm	Orders received to his BA to be prepared to move into action next day.	
	23rd	11 am	A Battery only, went into action with 150 TBde under Lt Col H ROCHFORT-BOYD. B Battery new HQ new MONTAUBAN village. (Map reference A.2.B. Sheet 62 C N.W.)	
	25		2 Lieut C W WILLIAMSON joined the Brigade and posted to C Battery. B. B Battery moved into action near Artillery	
	27 26		C Battery's supply of ammunition to A and B Batteries from 6 pm on 27th till 8 am on the 29th	20000

Original

Army Form C. 2118

WAR DIARY
or
INTELLIGENCE SUMMARY

167 Brigade R.F.A.

(Erase heading not required.)

Instructions regarding War Diaries and Intelligence Summaries are contained in F. S. Regs., Part II. and the Staff Manual respectively. Title Pages will be prepared in manuscript.

Place	Date	Hour	Summary of Events and Information	Remarks and references to Appendices
	28		A and B Batteries move up to closer range behind LONGUEVAL	
	29		Casualties 2 O.R. wounded.	
	30		4. O.R. wounds in A Battery	

J.H.C Gay Lieut / Adjt.
for Lieut-Col Comdg 167 Bde

Headquarters
33rd Divnl Artillery

Herewith War Diary for
167th Brigade RFA, now absorbed
into 156, and 162nd Brigades.

JHClong
12/9/16   Lieut & adjt
             for O/C 167th Bde RFA

WAR DIARY
INTELLIGENCE SUMMARY

167 / Brigade R.F.A.
Vol 8

33

Army Form C. 2118

Place	Date	Hour	Summary of Events and Information	Remarks and references to Appendices
	SEPTEMBER			
	1st	4am	B. Battery and A Battery heavily shelled with gas and other shell	
			Casualties in B. Battery: Major D. Stewart, Capt C.H. Walker, Lieut Gt Stanley-Clark — gassed	
			8 O.R. gassed	
			2 O.R. killed	
			A Battery: 2 O.R. wounded	
		1pm	C Battery relieved B. Battery in action. B. Battery returned to DERNANCOURT.	
	2nd		N° 23004 Bomb H. Smith HQ/167 awarded Military Medal	
			N° 21132 Sergt Ht. Kennett B/167 " " "	
			N° 49049 Sergt W. Harwood (since killed in action) B/167 awarded Military Medal	
			N° 22315 Gunner F Barnes awarded Military Medal	
		11am	Lt Col C.G. Stewart takes over temporary Command of 166 Bde due vice Lt Col Murray wounded in action	
	5		One section of A and C Batteries relieved by section of New Zealand Artillery	
	6	10am	One section each of A and C Batteries relieved whole of B Battery and HQ pm	

Army Form C. 2118

WAR DIARY
or
INTELLIGENCE SUMMARY
(Erase heading not required.)

167 Brigade R.F.A.

Instructions regarding War Diaries and Intelligence Summaries are contained in F. S. Regs., Part II. and the Staff Manual respectively. Title Pages will be prepared in manuscript.

Place	Date	Hour	Summary of Events and Information	Remarks and references to Appendices
	6/7/16		Marched to LA NEUVILLE, near CORBIE. Remaining picture of A and C Batteries and Lt Col C.G. STEWART rejoins the Bde	
	7th	11am	Brigade marched to FLESSELLES via LAHOUSSOYE – BEHENCOURT – MOLLIENS AU BOIS – VILLERS BOCAGE – BEHENCOURT. Lieut W.G. PRINGLE posted to command B. Battery, 2nd Lieut B. FFEITCH " " B. Battery.	
	8th	9am	Brigade marched to LE QUESNIL – OCCOCHES LE PETIT via CANAPLES – BERNAVILLE. Watered horses 1 mile S of CANAPLES. Arrived at 3 pm. HQ billeted at MON-PLAISIR. A Battery " LA QUESNIL Farm. B " " } " OCCOCHE LE PETIT C " " }	
	8/9/16	12 md	33° Div transferred to XVII Corps III Army from IV Army XV Corps	
	9th	11am	Brigade marched via HEM – DOULLENS – BOUT-DES-PRES, when it billeted for night.	
	10th	6:50 am	Brigade marched via LUCHEUX – BARLY – FOSSEUX – WANQUETIN to MONTENESCOURT	

WAR DIARY or INTELLIGENCE SUMMARY

Army Form C. 2118

167 Brigade RFA

Place	Date	Hour	Summary of Events and Information	Remarks and references to Appendices
	11th	1 am	Where it waited in the open. Orders received that 167 Bde would be broken up to form 6 gun 18 P batteries & in 166 Bde - 156 Bde - 162 Bde. (First army No SG 447/142). To be completed by 12 noon 12th inst.	
		9 pm	Capt B. FETHERSTON } receive MILITARY CROSS Lieut R.S.S. MITCHELL } A and ½ B Batteries to 156 Bde RFA. C " " " " 162 Bde RFA. Capt. S. TALBOT 2Lieut. W.G. SHEEREN } to 156 " C.A. BLDOR. } Bde. from A Battery " A.C. DAWES. " O.E. GALLIE Lieut Q.W.C. PRINGLE 2Lieut R.S.S. MITCHELL } to 156 Bde from B Battery 2Lieut G.W. WILLIAMSON 2Lieut. J.R. BARNES } To 162 Bde " D. FITCH } from B Battery Capt. G. FETHERSTON. Lieut J.R.G. TURNER. " A.R. TUCKER } to 162 Bde " J.H.K. PAYSON } from C Battery " J.C.J. CHAPMAN	Lt. Col. C.G. STEWART CMG DSO } to 166 Bde Lieut. J. CAMPBELL } from HQ Lt. Cmy. Lieut RFA. Ag. 167 Bde Ano.y.

1875 Wt. W593/826 1,000,000 4/15 J.B.C. & A. A.D.S.S./Forms/C. 2118.

www.ingramcontent.com/pod-product-compliance
Lightning Source LLC
Chambersburg PA
CBHW081242170426
43191CB00034B/2011